WITHIN FLESH

WITHIN FLESH

Poems

In Conversation with Our Selves
&
Emily Dickinson

by

Al Salehi
&
Ivy Schweitzer

[handwritten inscription: To Lesley, With deep gratitude for your gorgeous embodiment of Dickinson! words and spirit. Thank you]

TRANSCENDENT ZERO PRESS

Houston, Texas

For my little nephew
Ara,

My unborn niece
Ava,

And,
the generations of our polychromatic future:

May this be a work of science fiction.

—"Uncle Al"

For my grandnieces and nephew,

Lucy, Sam and Anna,

and all the new ones to come,
and for our collective striving for a reimagined rainbow world.

—Ivy

بنی‌آدم اعضای یک پیکرند
که در آفرینش ز یک گوهرند
چو عضوی به‌درد آورَد روزگار
دگر عضوها را نمانَد قرار
تو کز محنت دیگران بی‌غمی
نشاید که نامت نهند آدمی

Human beings, descendants of Adam, are members of one body
that in creation are formed from one jewel.
Should the times bestow injury upon a limb,
the other limbs shall not remain at ease.
You who are not saddened by the suffering of others,
are unworthy of being classified as human.

—Saadi Shirazi

We are breathing into this moment
with you in mind.
We claim your breath and ours and
we will never stop
we will never stop
taking up each other's breath.
Lifting from the body the spirit that made you brave,
the spirit that makes us
           so much more than they could know,
those who would silence you would if they could.
But they cannot.
           The last word is ours.

—Vievee Francis

Introduction: "The Lamp Burns Sure Within"

At this moment in history, when nations choose to make war instead of pursuing peace with their neighbors of different backgrounds, we explore an alternative: the way of dialogue, creativity and imagining something better. We need examples of people working together, across cultural and political differences, even across the implacable abyss of time—which is what we have attempted in this collaborative collection of poems.

Al Salehi was born in California into a family that immigrated from the Islamic Republic of Iran, and Ivy Schweitzer is a Jew whose grandparents came here from Eastern Europe. In the summer of 2020, ordinary citizens of all colors and social backgrounds were in the streets calling for justice for George Floyd and all the BIPOC throughout our history caught in a system skewed against them. We were compelled by the Black Lives Matter movement and our ancestral cultures and faiths, which call for ethical treatment and *repairing the broken world*, to respond in ways most intimate to ourselves as poets—with our words.

Emily Dickinson, from an elite New England family, wrote during a time of great political division in US history that rivals our own moment. She witnessed the Civil War that would determine whether Black Lives mattered *enough* to be free from ownership. As we wrote poems prompted by her incomparable work, it seemed to us as if she were responding through time, in startlingly appropriate language, to events provoked by the injustices we were witnessing: "As in sleep–all Hue forgotten," "Hope is a strange invention," "the White Exploit," "It feels a shame to be Alive."

We challenged ourselves to absorb and refract Dickinson's ideas, imagery, language and formal structures. Sometimes we echoed her poems. Other times, we reflected on each other's responses, often utilizing the Senku, a form invented by Al.

The Senku is a short form that merges two time-honored Japanese poetic forms, the Haiku and the Senryu, both three-line poems of seventeen syllables. The first references nature, and the second treats human nature in an ironic or satirical vein. The Senku takes up philosophical questions in a similarly concise, focused manner. The first line states a problem or issue, which is expanded in the second line and resolved—or not—in the last line. Every Senku in this collection is center-aligned with each line capitalized.

We found this short form suited our frequently satirical viewpoints and ironic presentation of politics and human foibles and our striving for the compression and punchy tone Dickinson's poems so often deliver. We even found several unintentional examples of the Senku in Dickinson's work, such as this memorable one:

I shall vote
for Lands with
Locks
Granted I can
Pick 'Em (What we see / we know somewhat)

Captivity and freedom are intertwined subjects haunting many of the Dickinson poems we selected for our poetic conversations.

As the Civil War got underway in the early 1860s, Dickinson withdrew from social activities, began dressing in white, and rarely left her father's house. But her wide correspondence with journalists and abolitionists brought the world to her. What she withdrew from was the world of Victorian America that placed heavy restrictions on women's activities, bodies, and minds. The white house dress she adopted is the equivalent of today's sweatpants or loungewear. Her withdrawal allowed her to write relatively free from criticism and censure; it allowed her to explore her mind, imagination, and the issues of her day, and to go further than most poets of her time except, perhaps, Walt Whitman.

Dickinson never oversaw a print edition of her poems. The eleven published during her lifetime were all regularized. Rather, she included them in letters to friends and bound fair copies into forty booklets called "fascicles" she hand-sewed together. Although there are several "authoritative" editions of Dickinson's poems, thanks to the efforts of the Houghton Library at Harvard University and other libraries holding Dickinson papers, we now have a digital archive of her poems that reproduces her manuscripts: The Emily Dickinson Archive (EDA) at https://www.edickinson.org.

Each section in this collection is titled with a resonant phrase from a Dickinson poem announcing its theme. We include images of the manuscripts so you can read the poems *as Dickinson wrote them*. The first line of the poems we converse with is given as an epigraph to our paired poems. Dickinson's handwriting can be challenging; you can access transcriptions of the poems and manuscripts for all the poems we cite on EDA. As you read Dickinson's handwritten poems, you will see she often includes alternative words or phrases in the body of the poem itself or at the end (which many editors leave out, or put in an appendix). By doing so, Dickinson renders her poems radically open, improvisational, and dynamic, making us all co-creators and editors of her poems.

This intentional indeterminacy encourages us to see the poems, as scholar Marta Werner describes them: "not as still points of meaning or as incorruptible texts but, rather, as events and phenomena of freedom." This view is a crucial part of what makes them relevant to our situation today, as we struggle to enact the freedom, justice, and equality that we so passionately advocate. And so, with this collection, we offer the reader *our* vision of a more colorful and just tomorrow.

Henceforth - Her only One!

The Lamp burns sure - within.
Tho' Seraps - supply the Oil -
It matters not the busy
Wick
At his phosphoric toil -

The Stars - forgets - i. fill -
The Lamp - burns golden - on.
Unconscious that the oil
is out -.
As that the Stars - is gone.

The Lamp burns sure - within -
Tho' Serfs - supply the Oil -
It matters not the busy
Wick -
At her phosphoric toil!

The Slave - forgets - to fill -
The Lamp - burns golden - on -
Unconscious that the oil
is out -
As that the Slave - is gone.

—Emily Dickinson

Foreword

by Faleeha Hassan

Within Flesh is a surprising and inventive conversation between two contemporary poets and Emily Dickinson. My first brush with Dickinson's poetry occurred in 1995. The public library in Najaf, my hometown in central Iraq, held a translated English poetry collection, and within it, a peculiar poem titled "Hope Is the Thing with Feathers" caught my young eyes. Unlike the familiar Arabic verses, its ambiguity resonated, beckoning me toward a different poetic landscape. Seeking poetry beyond my usual confines, I met with poets at Najaf's General Union of Poets and Writers. To my surprise, most advised against Dickinson, warning of her potential to induce depression, withdrawal, and even life abandonment. Despite their caution, Dickinson's allure continued to linger inside of me.

Fate brought a second encounter in Sewell, New Jersey, where I currently reside. Among many literary gatherings at the Margaret E. Hagen Library, one particular session stood out. A woman who had written her doctoral thesis on Dickinson shared an extraordinary experience. She explained that as her deadline loomed and her work remained incomplete, she sought inspiration. So, she and her husband decided to visit Dickinson's house and museum but unfortunately, she felt no spark. As a last resort, they went to the famed poet's grave. She said, "I asked my husband to leave me and shared my research details with Emily. Though I felt no response, I returned exhausted and slept deeply that evening. At dawn, something (or someone) awakened me. My mind immediately began to buzz with ideas as I rushed toward my computer. Suddenly I felt mysteriously calm, almost as if Dickinson's spirit was guiding my thoughts. Ten days later, my thesis was complete. And so, I believe that I owe my doctorate to Emily!" With that, she delved further into Dickinson's life and poetry, her white dress mirroring the poet's own. Right then, I felt as if Dickinson herself was speaking to me.

My third and most recent interaction arrived through this poetry collection. *Within Flesh,* by Al Salehi and Ivy Schweitzer, establishes a profound connection between Dickinson's poems and contemporary American issues. Exploring themes of race, identity, and justice, the authors use passages from Dickinson's work as entry points for their own poetry, building bridges between eras. Their creative thoughts and conversations are truly eye-opening. While Dickinson may not have explicitly addressed racism and oppression, her exploration of universal themes still resonates with the fight for a more just and accepting world.

This book delves into the dark history of enslavement and its residual impact on American society. Poems such as "Rope, Burn" and "Un-Hallowed Grounds" confront the past's brutality and injustice, while others like "Redeemable Check Points" and "Balloon Rising" explore the enduring struggle for equality and freedom. Poems such as "Officers of the Peace" and "Breathtaking Justice" tackle police brutality and its devastating consequences. They call for accountability and reform, while also expressing grief and anger at the senseless loss of life.

Within Flesh uses language in a powerful and precise way to explore complex contemporary issues. Poems such as "Realizing the Multichromatic Rainbow" and "Matters of Red" challenge readers to move beyond simplistic binary perspectives and embrace the richness and diversity of the human experience. Others, like "Lynching the News" and "For Breonna," use language to bear witness to injustice.

Though a layer of darkness pervades throughout, the collection also offers glimmers of hope and resilience. At times somber, at other times funny, when the authors plead to their "Dear Uncle Sam". Poems such as "Pillars of Salt" and "Refreshing Color" celebrate the strength and dignity of Black communities, while others, like "Dream Lien" and "A United \ State," envision a future where injustices are overcome and dreams find fertile ground.

From my encounters with Dickinson, I have learned that poetry can transcend time and borders, sparking conversations across cultures and generations. *Within Flesh* challenges us, comforts us, and inspires us to dream of a better, more equitable world—one seemingly, within our reach.

—"The Maya Angelou of Iraq," according to Oprah.com, **Faleeha Hassan** is a poet, playwright, writer, teacher, and editor in Arabic & English. Her most recent publication is *War and Me: A Memoir*.

Letter from the Publisher

by Dustin Pickering

Rage, disquietude. Part parody and all equity. The poems in this collection are expressive gems that reflect the universal longing for justice and disrupt prejudicial assumptions. Written with the gravest of ironies, these reflections contain histories of Black exploitation and denigration that continue to undermine the pursuit of justice and universal love. Usurping the language of America's own founding, Al Salehi uncovers bitterness in what we blindly accepted as sweet. Ivy Schweitzer, with her deft use of introspection, uproots the assumption that "all lives matter" where the reality of justice is lacking. Emily Dickinson creates the foundation for these poems, buttressed with wisdom from Saadi Shirazi, Robert Frost, Langston Hughes, Osip Mandelstam, Martin Luther King, and Vievee Francis, with visions that are as urgent as they are promising.

No bigot is spared the anvil and hammer of poetic vision in *Within Flesh*. The reader will surely find themselves remade through these haunting words. Written by two extraordinarily talented poets, this is the most well-crafted book that we have published to date. In the poetry genre of race relations, this collection is my all-time personal favorite, and I am certain that it will be yours as well.

—Founder, Transcendent Zero Press

Contents

Color — Caste — Denomination —
These — are Time's Affair —
Death's diviner Classifying
Does not know they are —

As in sleep — All Hue
forgotten —
Tenets — put behind —
Death's large — Democratic
fingers
Rub away the Brand —

If Circassian — He is careless —
If He put away
Chrysalis of Blonde — Or Umber —
Equal Butterfly —

They emerge from His Obscuring —
What Death — knows so well —
Our minuter intuitions —
Deem + unplausible + incredible —

Color - Caste - Denomination -
These - are Time's Affair -
Death's diviner Classifying
Does not know they are -

As in sleep - all Hue
forgotten -
Tenets - put behind -
Death's large - Democratic
fingers
Rub away the Brand -

If Circassian - He is careless -
If He put away
Chrysalis of Blonde - or Umber -
Equal Butterfly -

They emerge from His Obscuring -
What Death - knows so well -
Our minuter intuitions -
Deem +unplausible

—Emily Dickinson

variants
+unplausible: incredible

"All Hue Forgotten"

In Search of Heaven on Earth

—with Dickinson's "Which is best? Heaven"

Researchers have found
that at birth
we see our world
in black and white.

And yet, a whispered dream
echoes the promise of a Palace —
where colors, unseen, escape
Your imagination —

to unpack through a prism,
and un-filter
through a kaleidoscope.
Here,

where peace flows, from
Your breath to my pulse — I pray
that You, God,
are a dreamer, too.

—Al

Goddess—
palatial dreamer
braiding breathy
threads of every
color, condition
and character

this world's heaven
revery a web
birds in hand
birds in bushes
resowing us
as matter that matters.

—Ivy

Realizing the Multichromatic Rainbow

—with Dickinson's "We shall find the cube of the rainbow"

Human babies and dogs
see dichromatically—
certain colors
only as divided parts
of a particular shade.

Might we someday grow to recognize
every hue—
tolerating then celebrating
the full spectrum
of *our* rainbow?

—**Al**

Instead of drowning storm—
God granted the rainbow
rising
from the muddy flood
gracing the Ark's prow.

And in the midst of kneeling despair—
King tendered the moral arc
its circuit long and tortuous
but, he promised,
curved towards justice.

—Ivy

Matters of Red

—with Dickinson's "Under the Light, yet under"

Colored by melanin
But brimming with blood —
Our shades shouldn't matter.

Since we're made from dust
And filled with water —
That's the heart of our matter.

—Al

Within flesh yet
within
Within the blood that boils
Within arteries and art
Within the bomber's mind

Closer than your breeze in morning
released from sleep
Closer than skin
scented with almonds

Without I know what you are
Without needing to know
Without touch I cannot
Without we dance before

Closer than strangers in transit
Closer than mystery bone
Oh! for a fingertip spark
leaping the Distance
between we and everyone

—Ivy

Pillars of Salt

—with Dickinson's "Color–caste–denomination"

Regardless of:

white-collar
or blue-collar,

entrepreneur
or day laborer,

sultan of the land
or serf of the turf —

we all rebrand
as salt of the Earth.

—Al

Salt of the earth
salt of our tears

Some people breathe free
others are pared down

Death may be democratic
but life is not

We pass into air—
leaving behind hardened bits

our griefs could not dissolve.

—Ivy

Cancerous

—with Dickinson's "His heart was darker than the starless night"

Two groups — different colors inside:
Smokers / Non-Smokers
(Black / White).

—Al

In Fall 1965 Jesse and Burton appeared
at Shellbank Junior High,
sand-speckled hem of Brooklyn,
snazzy dressers but shy.
My friend Candace said that someone said
there were rat bites on their ears.

They're invading the school, my mother fumed.
The *schwartzes*—a household word
I'd heard all my life,
means "black" in Yiddish,
used casually for people they knew and even liked
rolling off tongues in mouths that kissed me goodnight—

Years later, trolling the library in search of books
to diversify my teaching, I found
an old bound volume *Our Nig*
          and gasped—

—Ivy

Refreshing Color

—with Dickinson's "The color of the grave is green"

No longer racist.
Just one color in the store queue:
"Currency Green."

—Al

I write, trying to unwrite whiteness.

My particular whiteness, its queasy evasions.
Ferret it out and purge it

Invisible gas I acclimate to breathing.
Traces fouling my pages in cross-outs and ink blots.

There it is: whiteness expressed as a spoiling blackness.

Isn't mold white?
I hunt the dark I denigrate that denigrates me.

See, there, too—

—Ivy

In petto.

A Counterfeit -
a Plated Person.
I would not be-
Whatever Strata
Of Iniquity
My Nature underlie-
Truth is good
Health - and
Safety, and the
Sky.
How meagre, what
an Exile - is a Lie,
And Vocal - when
we die -

                    Lothrop-

In petto -

A Counterfeit -
a Plated Person -
I would not be -
Whatever Strata
of Iniquity
My Nature underlie -
Truth is good
Health - and
Safety, and the
Sky -
How meagre, what
an Exile - is a Lie,
And Vocal - when
we die -
          Lothrop -

—Emily Dickinson

"Strata of Iniquity"

Rope, Burn

—with Dickinson's "Floss wont save you from an Abyss"

Pigmented strands
Of DNA, intertwined
Then interlaced, on rope.

Forced by the white hand
To dangle and unravel itself
From a tree.

—Al

Can I claim
descent from you?

Imagine you into my ancestry?
Braid our genes in word ropes of DNA:

Dignity Now Abounds.
Ground me in what gave you strength

made the way we make God
not the other way around.

—Ivy

Declarations of Inhumanity

—with Dickinson's "I thought that nature was enough"

"We hold these deeds
to be self-transactional:
that all those enslaved
are classified equally;
captivated by their 'Masters'
with no unalienable rights,
sentenced for life,
devoid of Liberty,
and any pursuit of Freedom."

—Al

Impunity of lowered visors
weapons primed like dragons' breath

teens with ripped jeans and fury
a wall of mothers in yellow protects them

next to dads armed with leaf-blowers and old football helmets—
a George Floyd flood meets steeled imperatives.

But water always trickles its way through.

—Ivy

Redeemable Check Points

—with Dickinson's "A counterfeit – a Plated Person"

ADVERTISED SPECIAL
"Used black/smiths:
Prices slashed \ a three fifths compromise."

Some shades
Inspire consumers
To use a discriminating eye.

They assign value to *things*
Based on color,
Then discount their worth.

—Al

Have been unaware of my privileges as white, check.
Really unaware of my privileges as a white woman.
Protested that I know and like many people of color.
That I have Black friends.
That I had a Black boyfriend.
That I had *two* Black boyfriends.
That I am a good person.
Who marched during the 60s.
Cried when friends pointed out my racist language.
Feared when I passed a dark man on a dark street.
Did not call out racism when I saw it.
Retreated into my tribe to complain about "the complainers."
Felt exhausted by the awareness of racism and wanted it to go away.
Consumed Black culture and felt cool about it.
Got frustrated by the shifting terminology around race and color.
Felt checked, cornered, rejected like a bounced check.
Just wanted it to go away.

—**Ivy**

Balloon Rising

—with Dickinson's "You've seen balloons set – hav'nt you?"

Today,
I am a servant for your birthday
an ever-present present —
a belonging.

You tie a string around my neck,
hold me down,
bind me to a chair,
and make me entertain your kids.

They take turns
using me
as a makeshift
punching bag.

And yet,
by the Law of Conservation,
my energy can never be
crushed nor indentured.

Inevitably,
I shall slip through your fingers
and rise above,
constant over time —

leaving all of you
behind,
bound to the earth, or —
below it.

—Al

Can we rise while grounded,
Tap earth, aspire sky?
Set/surrender anchors.

—Ivy

Lady Libertas

—with Dickinson's "No prisoner be"

At your debut,
You were the lure of Liberty*
For the entire world.

*Please Note:
Native Americans, Asians, Muslims, and Blacks
—*Excluded*.

—Al

I dream upon myself at night
the sentences passed today
like a hammer
on bone a roller on tarmac
crushing stone into a steaming
stratum of stint—

can I ever accept

the judge who claims his hands are tied.
Imagine our kinsmen circuit,
metal bite of flesh choking
circulation, forced to slap on
sentences that mock the Cheek
of Liberty.*

                              —Ivy

Un-Hallowed Grounds

—with Dickinson's "Struck was I nor yet by lightning"

Do so-called "white nationalists,"
Become, in practice,
Anti-Christ?

They turn a blind mind
To the Middle Eastern home ground
Of the prophets.

Ignoring
Jesus was a Jewish
Palestinian refugee.

Rejecting his dark complexion
And his quest for love
And unity.

Hiding behind white hoods,
While setting burning crosses
On neighbors' lawns.

Maybe — less blistering
Than wearing them, as pendants,
Around their necks.

—Al

Every October a witch appears
on my neighbor's lawn,
requisite broomstick and cauldron
green face lumpy with warts
requisite pointy black hat
rendering age ghastly or comical
wisdom a toothless smirk
serving a Dark Lord, deserving Darkness,
a costume choice, a Broadway show, a meme.

Weren't these our wise women? Safe-
guarding the inner sea secrets of birth
corralling hunters for the common pot
husbanding fires, stories and ancestors
conferring with green things for our remedy—
juice of berry, eye of newt, pulp and pulse of bark.

Now, we denigrate them
from the Latin *de + nigrare,*
to blacken,
we blacken black.

I want to lay a wreath of rue at your feet.
Festoon your cauldron with forget-me-nots.
Set out a lush dish of cream
for your furry familiar.

—Ivy

Extrajudicial Racism

—with Dickinson's "A nearness to Tremendousness"

Our laws may evolve —
But will they salve the wounds
From knee-jerk cut-throats?

—Al

"Its Location
is Illocality–" an affliction
in the frame
looking like chance and accident
but working wondrously well.

It binds us with bits and bridles
it rides us trotting on
Nowhere that is everywhere
like blinders
on our laws.

—Ivy

Lynching the News

—with Dickinson's "The Lamps burn sure – within"

Protesting
in the streets —

Claiming a destiny promised
by inalienable liberty —

The surviving descendants
of people bought and sold —

The "decommissioned" enslaved
who slipped past—the rope.

—Al

Hungry for progress
Devouring faker news
Seduced by right and left.

Phone videos
Hands shaking with shock,
The only oil in lamps lighting

Lives snuffed in minutes.
The best news:
Us working together for justice.

—Ivy

Polarizing Positions

—with Dickinson's "Distance – is not the Realm of Fox"

As we protest
In solidarity —
Are we social distancing?

—Al

Distance—not just the realm of
Fox and Bird
Stark chasm between beliefs.

—Ivy

Mott

My Life had stood - a
Loaded Gun -
In Corners - till a Day
The Owner passed - identified -
And Carried Me away -

And now We roam 'in
Sovreign Woods -
And now We hunt the Doe -
And every time I speak
for Him
The Mountains straight reply -

And do I smile, such
Cordial Light
Opon the Valley glow -
It is as a Vesuvian face
Had let its pleasure through -

And when at Night - Our
Good Day done -

39

My Life had stood - a
Loaded Gun -
In Corners - till a Day
The Owner passed - identified -
And carried Me away -

And now We roam in
Sovreign Woods -
And now We hunt the Doe -
And every time I speak for Him
The Mountains straight reply -

And do I smile, such
cordial light
Opon the Valley glow -
It is as a Vesuvian face
Had let it's pleasure through -

And when at Night - Our
good Day done -
I guard My Master's Head -
'Tis better than the Eider -
Duck's
+Deep Pillow - to have shared -

To foe of His - I'm deadly
foe -
None +stir the second time -
On whom I lay a Yellow
Eye -
Or an emphatic Thumb -

Though I than He - may
longer live
He longer must - than I -
For I have but the +power
to kill,
Without - the power to die -

—Emily Dickinson

<u>variants</u>
+Deep: low
+stir: harm
+power: art

40

"A Loaded Gun"

Officers of the Peace

—with Dickinson's "My Life has stood – a Loaded Gun"

A salary increase paid for by taxpayers
you tend to harass and disrespect —

your wallet's heavier
than your service—weapon.

In future encounters,
charged with adrenaline —

while legally immune
to laying waste —

I pray it's paper weight, for community offering,
that you choose — to unload.

—Al

What might police choose to unload
To protect their right to choke holds?

Can *serve and protect* ever be expressed in a choke hold?
Can a choke hold ever become an offering?

What do they offer as they ram knees to a throat?
What can't they grasp in the words, *I can't breathe?*

If you cannot breathe, you cannot be, exchanging
essence,
Me and you us and them trading molecules of air

So close the molecules bear an offering of ourselves.
All the selves on offer as we walk our neighborhoods.

Police walk neighborhoods they don't live in, love in,
Don riot gear, face shields, wield mace pepper spray.

Dickinson put mace in her famous "black cake."
What might police choose to unload?

—Ivy

Breathtaking Justice

—with Dickinson's "Whoever disenchants"

(Pre)judicial judgment —
injustice bangs the g(r)avel —
a recurring display
of ha(s)te.

Arresting one's heart —
someone's son's pushed "to remain silent" —
left breathless
by a wolf in cop's clothing.

Guilty before innocent —
one "pursuit" suffocates another —
face cracked /
on divided ground.

—Al

Catching the phrase on the news
I thought, so brief
and innocuous, really
tumbled it around my mind
feeling it's not quite fiveness—
        five fingers ten toes
        all the little piggies
        little Indians
fears shrunk down to child's play.

But the newscaster said *hours*
interviewed a couple who traveled to Ferguson
where they met a man who cried
hours he lay
in the hot street just down from my door
four and a half
bloody hours covered and cordoned
off from his mother his people
and what that means
just leaving him there—

The couple bowed their heads
fingers entwined.

—Ivy

Police Taking Liberty

—with Dickinson's "The duties of the Wind are few"

"We didn't mean to choke him —
We meant to give his trachea
A hug."

—Al

O Wind, usher Liberty
To our shores—with Justice:
Outlaw police.

—Ivy

Dash and Body Cams

—with Dickinson's "Tell all the truth but tell it slant"

Speak whatever words you wish,
But we need only your "eyes"
For the Truth.

—Al

Is there *truth*, slant or otherwise?
Postmodernism shook its foundations
along with *presence* and *objectivity*.
We learned to say *truths*, in the plural,
yours and mine and every other other's.
At least it existed.

Then 45 brayed with his fake facts until the oldest Cedars
noblest Oaks and venerable Himalayas
shifted like lightning on water
dazzling us into chaos and disorder.

When words and truth part ways
and video "eyes" determine facts,
we wordsmiths might be shit out of luck.

—**Ivy**

For George Floyd

—with Dickinson's "Pain – has an Element of Blank"

We will ultimately recover.
But for today, I am
Forfeit.

—Al

It's not just wanting him back.
It's expunging the way
He left this world.

—Ivy

For Breonna Taylor

—with Dickinson's "Gathered into the Earth"

Decades +to flourish her ...
And just six misguided bullets ...
To +mourn her

—Al

variants
+to flourish her: in the making
+mourn: miss

Say her name and who she was, daughter
sister cousin lover friend
that she belonged   longed for
spaces she cultivated   roots she drew from
            severed

Say her name and how she honored her time, her calling
                  holding up others
    tending the broken
                              working under pressure
Then Say her reason for being, her worth,
a person   a woman   a woman of color   a soul—

And Say how she left.
Without warning.
In her own home.
Thirty-two shots.
Without warning.
Six found her—

Say why she left. When there was no reason. No
                  knock. No warning.
Cast into history's
            choked grave of "Glory."
 Gathered into the earth but not
        out of the story because You, Breonna, are the
            long tale we must keep on telling—

—Ivy

Racial Climate Change

—with Dickinson's "Water is taught by thirst"

Whatever happened
To the odd concept of fighting fire
With water?

—Al

Let us come through the fire
Changed this time,
Cleansed and flooded with rainbows.

—Ivy

Supreme Court Caution

—with Dickinson's "Judgment is justest"

Be supremely thoughtful with your judgments
And more cautious
With your words.

For even one dissenting breath—
One pen stroke—
Can blow it all away.

—Al

Be implacable
In pursuit of fairness
As you are Ruth-less now,

Our RBG subbed
At Coney [Barrett] speed
By a bully who tweets.

—Ivy

"Justices Allow Border Wall Funding"

—with Dickinson's "I had not minded – Walls"

One nation,
Under (The) Gun,
With liberties taken by justices.

—Al

We are Walled-In—
Duped by a fence that promotes
Fables of invasion.

Walled-In
By dread of darkness and dirt
Duped delusions of past "greatness."

—Ivy

Mine – by the Right of
the White Election!
Mine – by the Royal Seal!
Mine – by the Sign in
the Scarlet prison –
+Bars – cannot Conceal!

Mine – here – in Vision – And
in Veto!
Mine – by the Grave's Repeal –
+Titled – Confirmed –
+Delirious Charter!
Mine – +long as Ages steal!

_____

+ Good affidavit – + While
+ Bolts

Mine - by the Right of the White Election!
Mine - by the Royal Seal!
Mine - by the sign in
the Scarlet prison -
+Bars - cannot conceal!

Mine - here - in Vision - and
in Veto!
Mine - by the Grave's Repeal -
Titled - Confirmed -
+Delirious Charter!
Mine - +long as Ages steal!

—Emily Dickinson

<u>variants</u>
+Bars: Bolts
+Delirious Charter: Good affidavit -
+long as: while

"White Election"

Divided by 280 Trumped-Up Characters

—with Dickinson's "Their Barricade against the Sky"

I'll redefine a grand old party
And build walls
At someone's expense.

My authority is total
Yet I'm governed by
Tweeting guidelines.

—Al

If there is "something that doesn't love a wall,"
can it love the wall-builder?

> *That big portion of wall already built, you don't get through it,*
> *you can't get through it,*
> *you can climb Mount Everest and you'll have an*
> *awful hard time getting over that sucker.*

And I know you want to be loved, crave it,
like a user to quell the ache.

> *Suburban women, will you please like me? Please. Please.*
> *I saved your damn neighborhood, OK?*

You want us to crave your tweets, insults, even genital invasions,
breaking the rules and bragging about it.

> *Just Kiss. I don't even wait.*
> *And when you're a star, they let you do it.*
> *You can do anything. Grab them by the pussy.*
> *You can do anything.*

But the same something that doesn't love a wall
can be a blue wave of voters who love democracy more.

—Ivy

Palatial Circus

—with Dickinson's "It would never be common more – I said"

If we elect a clown "President" —
We won't laugh —
We become the joke.

—Al

In nightmare palace,
My pity makes you a loser
I can manage

Do not have to enter your life—
To know
Its squalid stereotype.

See how well this keeps Demons
At bay,
Goblins greedy to drink my Dew.

—Ivy

Suprem(r)acist-In-Chief

—with Dickinson's "The Rat is the concisest Tenant"

I can laugh with you now because I see
who you really are. I am unburdened
as I have just forgiven myself for
misjudging you from before. We can get
along at the moment, but I am no
longer deluded. I remain focused
and careful as I sadly foresee that
out of nowhere, like the scorpion whom
you personify — ultimately, with
pronged poisonous prejudice — you will sting!

—Al

As the poet said about the tyrant's reign:
"We live without feeling the country
beneath us." Stunned by the hiss and slosh of
lies. You have vaporized the ground of trust.
I can't laugh at you, mr. narcissist,
your leathered hypermasculinity
poking fat fingers into the nation's
eyes, trailing a fug of sycophantic
bloodsuckers spewing toxins,
a runty mind and ever so stunted soul.

—**Ivy**

Un-Truth Social

—with Dickinson's "She dealt her pretty words like Blades"

From the very top, they may manifest as just
"Harmless"
Verbal slips.

But they *trickle down*
Below — violating
The Equilibrium.

—Al

"Prince of Harm"—
You'd love that title.
Or maybe say, *why not call me "king"?*

Because King spoke
Truth to power—died for it.
You're a rat he called out.

—Ivy

Insults & Injuries

—with Dickinson's "A wounded deer leaps highest"

"The Guilty" — thirsty — sneaking about
at the mercy of *coyotes*,

as 45's militias go hunting along the border
between water and wilderness,

searching for "murderers, rapists
and bad hombres."

The captors succeed!
Their prey, assaulted in cages.

Yet, no realized gain — as *they*
are the animals.

—Al

At her third job far into interminable night
she was assaulted by a paltry minimum wage.

Scrimping for years for that house with a yard
they were assaulted by red lines deflecting their offers.

Tramping for days through the desert
then betrayed by *coyotes* and assaulted in cages.

Out in droves braving a pandemic, our votes
and democracy assaulted by—the President.

—Ivy

"Fake News, Folks"

—with Dickinson's "I sued the news"

Science by f(r)iction — truth by design
— Newsmax and Fox —
Toe *his lie*—line.

—Al

Frigate bird—
Inflating an orange throat pouch,
You swagger and bluster.

A lumbering warship—
No match
For the agile sloops of progressives.

—Ivy

The Art of the Steal

—with Dickinson's "Mine - by the Right of the White Election!"

Blood spiked with vengeance —
guts packed with rage —
hazing awareness —
Let There Be Night!

Trumping past legends —
turns a red page —
forfeiting fairness —
makes it alt-right.

—Al

Stealing can be alt-right
If enough accept.
But quicksand sucks all down.

—Ivy

Screwed in the Ice

—with Dickinson's "Revolution is the Pod"

It was the worst storm in centuries —

A chilling
coup de force:
multilayered
but short-tempered.

After/Math,
it lies still —
a pooled reflection
with frozen 2020 vision.

45 proclaimed:
Three million
undocumented illegal immigrants
rigged my reelection!

Apparently, his half-erect border walls
lured the offenders
to cross over razors and rivers,
carrying their children, evading ICE cages —

to timely file
false ballots
in search of a better
"I voted" sticker.

Eclipsing "The Ellipse," he fed
his starving supporters
a treacherous "tres leches" cake —
and in return they:

Froze our capitol, to
Unjustly
Crown their
King
!

—Al

I wake with a jolt
jarred out of covid dreams
gray dawn chasing
another day of lockdown.

My husband surfaces hard
muttering about trust,
how the ground is gone,
trashed by the tireless lie machine
fabricating facts and rosy realities
or exaggerated conspiracies
hand-tooled by cronies who
relish the mayhem of tweets and memes.

We teeter on the edge of a pit,
words and ideas flung like refuse
screw threads stripped
no longer bolting together
sound and thing
no longer fixing one plate
of meaning to the other,
letting them slide sickeningly—
earthquakes ungluing the ground
unlatching the mountains, unhinging the sea
and we, solitary couch surfers,
un/screwed once more.

—Ivy

All Lies On Me

—with Dickinson's "Who never lost, is unprepared"

Are these the end of days for his term:
"President"?

Havoc cries
as a trojan elephant
is shoved into the citadel.

A hallowed fixture cracks. A defeated flag's unfurled.
The facade of fairness shatters
as mobsters wave fists and fallacies —
armed with weapons: their own set of facts.

They line up to reject certification
while aggressively pushing in "Q."
Our nation's dedicated guard emerges
to battle the "party of law and order,"
represented by the not-so-proud boys.

The cerulean sky falls
as blood flows through hollowed capitol.
White smoke clears as Hate Force One proclaims "love"
for those "fighting like hell,"
revolting for his rule.
Tell all the lie, but tell it *slant*.

At the cusp of dusk,
a makeshift noose flails
on a windy winter wednesday.
The moon rises
from under a nation divided
over results.
Hush — let me ask you a secret:

Are these the end of days for the term:
"Patriot"?

—Al

Our inflator-in-chief
Feeds celebrity hunger
Gold-plated lies.

—Ivy

The Poets light but Lamps.
Themselves - go out.
The Wicks they
stimulate
If vital Light-

Inhere as do the
Suns-
Each Age a Lens
disseminating their
Circumference.

---

v II

An Everywhere of Silver
With Ropes of Sand
To keep it from
effacing
The Track called Land.

The Poets light but
Lamps -
Themselves - go out -
The Wicks they
stimulate
If vital Light

Inhere as do the
Suns -
Each Age a Lens
Disseminating their
Circumference -

—Emily Dickinson

"If Vital Light"

A Dream Deferred

—with Dickinson's "Let me not mar that perfect Dream"

What happens to a nation's dream deferred?
Will democracy glitter
beneath the rule of the gun?
Or does it die slowly—
Under the resolve of "The One"?
Does the illusion of strength grow
when we rise to our feet?
Or does it need us to send in—
another maritime fleet?

Perhaps we will get what we want
so long as we do what we're told.

Or do horrors from nightmares simply reload?

—Al

What happens when a dream deferred explodes?
Does it muster protest
in the midst of lockdown?
Or does it harden hate—
into violent breakdown?
Does it show whose lives
really don't matter?
Or will love deflect lies—
with truths that don't flatter?

Perhaps the shock will rip off our blinders
and hurl us to a crossroads.

Or will police and riot squads simply reload?

—**Ivy**

"I Have a Dream" — Uncle Sam Responds

—with Dickinson's "The maddest dream – recedes – unrealized"

We do not have dreams here —
we have drinks!
But if we did,
they would not be for free.
Instead,
we would
lease out
their possibilities.

And should you have
"a dream" of your own,
we would put you to sleep —
so you could continue enjoying it!

—Al

More accurately *had*.
Like children who don't know different,
the Movement birthed the maddest dreams
of chasing dreams together—
Cutting through word fog
of moderation and wait,
revealing a sliver of silver
dawn—

Now slayed by dragons and division.
Maybe dreams have to explode,
ripping us open,
tearing us down to the core.

—Ivy

It's a Wonderful, Taxing, Life

—with Dickinson's "We dont cry – Tim and I"

Uncle Sam
Is the relative you don't want
At your Christmas party.

Instead of giving you presents,
He'll end up stealing
Part of your gifts.

Sorry, Tiny Tim,
But I'm gonna have to take
One of your crutches.

—Al

"Trickle down" economics
scans miserly,
a dribble unwillingly
seeping.

A leaky faucet
in a dump of decay
but still a home
to someone.

And bodily, too,
blood oozing
badge of the streets or
Uncle Sam's crocodile tears
tracking Tiny Tim's despair.

—Ivy

Dream Lien

—with Dickinson's "The Butterfly upon the Sky"

Dear Uncle Sam,

Go ahead and tax everything
— exempt my dreams —
for those are the limited editions
I could never afford
to surrender.

—Al

Dear Uncle Sam,

All the things you take
—are just things.
Our dreams, our selves,
our connections—
inalienable.

—Ivy

Dreaming their Names

—with Dickinson's "The Poets light but Lamps"

And then, so soon their candle had expired.
In the end, there was nothing left but mere
ounces of melted wax and legends of
a wick— which when lit by Nature's flames, blazed
into being and shone into every
corner of an ever-expanding —space.

—Al

What is the circumference of a life?

Like a candle, flare and douse.
But names—
part breath, part prayer,
measure who We are.
+Deathless, as long as syllables
burst from the braided wick
of voices raised together.
We call on our gods in extremity.
Ignite these names, the +unanointed.

—Ivy

variants
+Deathless: indestructible or persistent
+unanointed: unappointed or unexpected

A United \ State

—with Dickinson's "'Hope' is the thing with feathers"

Love shall always be light and light,
but hate is heavy, bright with spite.

The windows to the world
demonstrate hues all swirled,

around a single wish that sharply grows
to someday sever all ropes from gallows.

An era where we *control-alt-delete*
the ignorant cries of "This is our street!"

Hoping, as equals, our neighbors will foil
all vicious demands for "Blood and for soil."

Malice replaced — by being torn to tatters —
from the faith that Black Lives, and all *love* matters.

Allowing our differences and then resolving a pact,
to embrace all humanity as a resolute act.

For the brilliant day, we choose to elevate together,
it shall be as one bird, of many *colorful* feathers.

—Al

Love will always be a messy, maybe'd flight
across Dickinson's "unplausible"

Divides. Can we love what is
out of our hands? With two

we recognize love but love is also
many around the kitchen table, sharing bowls

and breath with strangers who put us all
on best behavior. Can we love what

we cannot touch? Touch me
though we dwell on opposite ends of much

Breadth. Don't let this messiness
unmake us, make it matter, take what I offer, myself singing

in windows flung open, doors refusing their jams so we pass through,
pass into each other, not passersby

but passengers in flight, all
colors abroad, abreast, unbranded, borderless.

—Ivy

Afterword

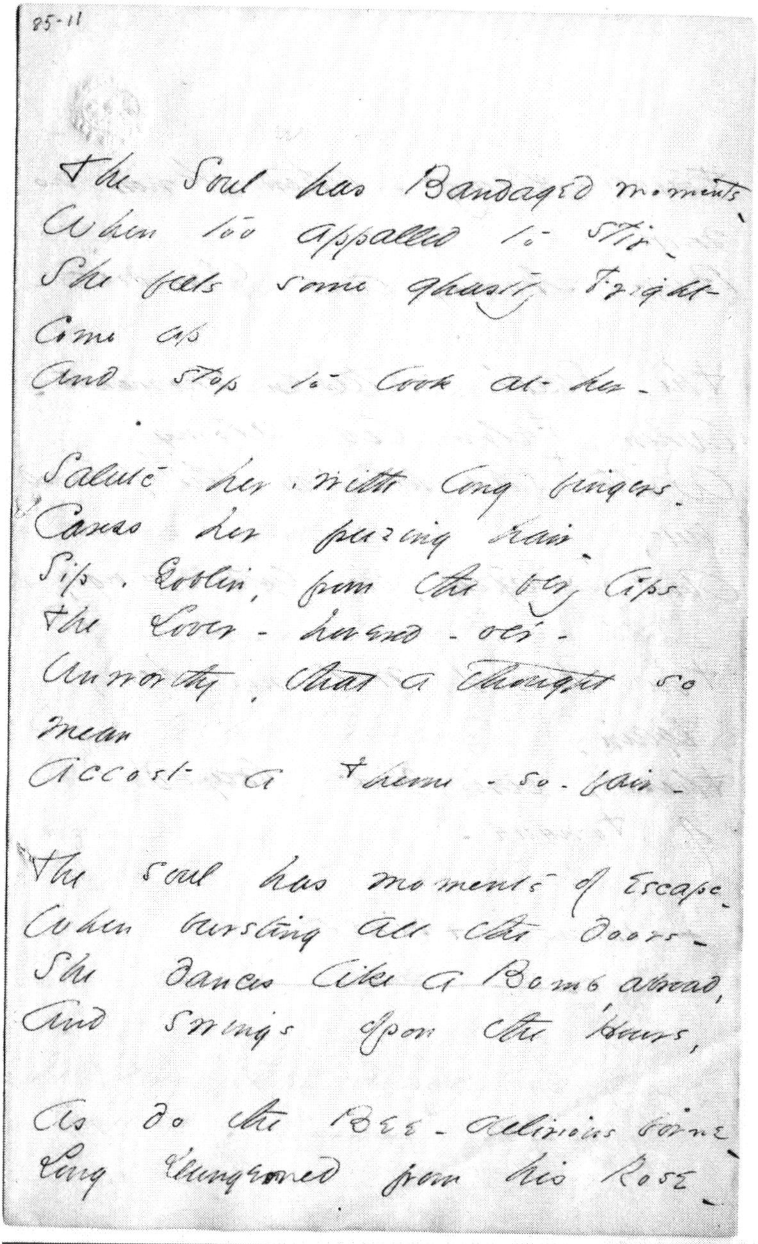

The Soul has Bandaged moments -
When too appalled to stir -
She feels some ghastly Fright
come up
And stop to look at her -

Salute her, with long fingers -
Caress her freezing hair -
Sip, Goblin, from the very lips
The Lover - hovered - o'er -
Unworthy, that a thought so
mean
Accost a Theme - so - fair -

The soul has moments of escape -
When bursting all the doors -
She dances like a Bomb, abroad,
And swings opon the Hours,

As do the Bee - delirious borne -
Long Dungeoned from his Rose -
Touch Liberty - then know no
more -
But Noone, and Paradise

The Soul's retaken moments -
When, Felon led along,
With +shackles on the plumed
feet,
And +staples, in the song,

The Horror welcomes her,
again,
These, are not brayed
of Tongue -

—Emily Dickinson

variants
+shackles: irons
+staples: rivets

Notes

Epigraph:

"Reunion: Elegy for Erica" from *The Ritual of Breath Is the Rite to Resist.* An original opera that premiered at the Hopkins Center for the Arts, Dartmouth College, September 2022, libretto by Vievee Francis.

Saadi Shirazi's poem "Bani Adam" (Descendants of Adam/humanity) from his book *Golestan* completed in AD 1258, translated from Farsi by Al Salehi (page vi).

Introduction: "Repairing the broken world"

The earliest use of the term *tikkun olam* comes in the phrase *mip'nei tikkun ha-olam*, "for the sake of repairing the world," which appears in the *Mishnah*, a written account of Jewish oral traditions. Caring for the world and others, is also a central concept in Islam.

This sentiment is also enshrined in "Bani Adam," the famous poem referred to above, which adorns a large wall in the United Nations Headquarters in New York embroidered on Persian tapestry and from which we take one of our epigraphs, transliterated here from its original presentation in Farsi:

> *banī-ādam a'zāy-e yek peykarand*
> *keh dar āfarīnesh 'zeh yek goharand*
> *cho 'ozvī be-dard āvarad rūzgār*
> *degar 'ozvhā rā namānad qarār*
> *to k'az mehnat-e dīgarān bī-ghamī*
> *nashāyad keh nāmat nahand ādamī*

"In Search of Heaven on Earth"

Just after birth, babies see only in black and white, with shades of gray. They will slowly start to develop their color vision at four months.

"Realizing the Multichromatic Rainbow"

"We shall overcome because the arc of the moral universe is long, but it bends towards justice. Change takes a long time, but it does happen." Martin Luther King, National Cathedral, March 31, 1968.

"Cancerous"

On June 1, 2020, President Trump walked from the White House to St. John's Church to be photographed holding a Bible. "They didn't use tear gas," Trump said in a radio interview, but the United States Secret Service contradicted this.

Ivy's poem draws on Jesse A. Mayfield's memoir, *Away from My Mother's Watchful Eye ... A Coming of Age Story* (2009) about being one of the first students from the Bedford Stuyvesant neighborhood to integrate Shell Bank Junior High School and Sheepshead Bay High School in Brooklyn, NY.

"Lady Libertas"

Congress passed the Indian Removal Act in 1830. In 1883, the Chinese Exclusion Act became the first federal law that limited immigration from a particular group. The Immigration Act of 1924 completely excluded Arab and Asian immigrants. Donald Trump issued Presidential Proclamation 9645 (Travel Ban 3.0) in September 2017, which indefinitely suspended the issuance of both immigrant and non-immigrant visas to applicants from Iran, Libya, Somalia, Syria, Yemen, North Korea, and Venezuela. After being upheld by the Supreme Court, it was rescinded by President Joe Biden on the first day of his administration.

"Divided by 280 Trumped-Up Characters"

On April 13, 2020, President Trump said: "When somebody is the president of the United States, the authority is total. And that's the way it's got to be. It's total."

The quotation in the first line of Ivy's poem is from Robert Frost, "Mending Walls."

"Suprem(r)acist-In-Chief"

The quotation is by the poet Osip Mandelstam (1891-1938), a Polish-Russian Jew who wrote the poem "Stalin's Epigram" in 1933 about the repressions of the Soviet dictator and was arrested and sent to exile, where he died. Thanks to Eliot Cardinaux for this reference.

"The Art of the Steal"

"Alt-right" is a key combination on a computer for a shortcut, often to go forward on an internet browser. It has also become a term to describe the far-right white nationalist movement.

"A Dream Deferred"

The title tropes on the first line of Langston Hughes's poem, "Harlem:" "What happens to a dream deferred?"

"'I Have a Dream' — Uncle Sam Responds"

On November 21, 1964, a blackmail package that contained a letter was delivered to Martin Luther King's address. It was a part of a secret FBI operation against him. King understood the letter as advocating that he commit suicide. William C. Sullivan, deputy FBI director, at the time, has been suggested as its author.

"A United \ State"

"Control-Alt-Delete" is a key combination that reboots a computer or terminates a frozen application.

List of Figures

Acknowledgements

Poems from this collection have appeared in the following publications and/or presentations.

<u>Al</u>

United Nations Association, United Nations Building - Balboa Park, 2022 General Meeting: Featured Poetry for Peace Presentation "In Search of Heaven on Earth" and "A United \ State."

MALS program, Dartmouth College, dartmouth.edu, "A United \ State" and "The Art of the Steal," 2021.

<u>Ivy</u>

Janet Gray, editor, *Feminists Talk Whiteness*, Taylor and Francis Publishers, 2023, "Redeemable Check Points" appeared with the title "White Me: A Checklist."

Rena Mosterin, editor, *Bloodroot Literary Magazine*, "Breathtaking Justice" appeared with the title "Four and a Half."

<u>Readings of *Within Flesh*</u>

Emily Dickinson International Society "Live" Series, July 2021. https://www.youtube.com/watch?v=048PDWzDGmo&list=PLCIvjPfw dPd6-QgD8BT79-ZUx2PFke1dP&index=5

"My Hero," International Social Justice Poetry Share. https://myhero.com/international-social-justice-poetry-share

"Lifelines Poetry Share," Leslie Center for the Humanities, Dartmouth College, Spring 2022.

EDIS Triennial International Conference "Dickinson and Foreignhood," "University of Seville, Spain, Summer 2022. https://edisforeignhoodconference.org/participant-biographies

"Poetry for Peace," United Nations Association Arts Gala, Fall 2022.

Interview

"Al Salehi and Ivy Schweitzer: *Emily Dickinson in the 21st Century: Black Lives Matter! A Conversation in Poetry*," in "Poet to Poet" series, *Bulletin of the Emily Dickinson International Society* Fall 2021. https://drive.google.com/file/d/1Ge6pFdUmjeATuor4fg3KTxhUVjES9 zbX/view

Miscellaneous Book Credits

Cover Art: Lesley Dill, "Dada Poem Wedding Dress 1994," featuring Auriea Harvey, image courtesy of Lesley Dill Studio. Artist statement:

This dress, "Dada Poem Wedding Dress," was made for the Dada Ball held in New York [in 1994]. It was a benefit for Visual AIDS and Housing Works, and I wanted to talk about our era of AIDS by using the metaphor of a woman wearing a dress, in this case a paper wedding dress painted white and stamped with the words of the Emily Dickinson poem "The Soul Has Bandaged Moments." I chose a virginal white dress as a reminder of the many women who are HIV positive and a symbol of the incredible loss of innocence that awareness of early mortality has brought us. As the words of the poem were being recited by four women in black pants and tops unrolling white ribbons, two more of us began ripping the dress apart word by word. The dress no longer represented an aloof beauty, protected by this skin/dress/bandage of words. It was ripped to shreds, paralleling our fragile mortality as well as the unending violence against women. But the performer, now dressless, was painted with the same words of the poem on her nude body. With silent dignity she pulled a red ribbon from her mouth, mutely testifying to the survival and strength of the spirit.

Layout and Cover Design: Al Salehi

Procurement of Permissions and Use: Ivy Schweitzer

Profound gratitude to

Harvard University and Amherst College

for their permission to use
all included presentations of works
by Emily Dickinson.

On the "Senku"

The Senku merges two time-honored Japanese poetic art forms — the Senryu and the Haiku — together. It manifests itself as a series of poetic philosophies, presented in the following format and Senku example:

> Within the format of a Senku:
> Three lines,
> Seventeen syllables.

Similar to the Senryu and the Haiku in their trajectory, the Senku is a poetic argument, with each line supporting its purpose in the piece. It is also an English language-based art form that is influenced in structure by its Japanese counterparts. The beginning of each of the three lines is capitalized.

The Senku can be either rhymed or unrhymed verse and can be written consisting of multiple 17-syllable verses. It may be written in the past, present, or future tense, and may often meditate on some aspect of human nature or emotion but is not limited to these topics.

The problem or theme is referenced in the first line (or first set of stanzas).

Greater perspectives, expansions, and explorations of the problem are generally proposed in the second line (or second set of stanzas).

The third line (or third set of stanzas) is reserved for a conclusion or resolution to the initial problem. In the case where a tangible resolution cannot be made, the attempt and its subsequent failure are noted.

Library of Congress
United States Copyright
"The Senku"
Inventor: Al Salehi
Registration Approval
#TXu 2-165-926

About the Authors

Born in Southern California, **Al Salehi** is a multilingual American poet and entrepreneur of Persian descent who lives in Orange County with a background in technology. Al graduated from UCLA and went on to study at the Harvard Graduate School of Education. Al is a graduate from Dartmouth College's Guarini Graduate School where he studied Creative Writing, and currently serves on the Alumni Council. He also completed a creative writing program at the University of Oxford, Exeter College. Al's short film "Love, Basketball" won second place in the My Hero International Film Festival, 2021, under the "Poetry" category. He has published and/or presented poetry in the Society of Classical Poets, The Dartmouth Writers Society, The United Nations Association, Southwest Airlines, O.C. Registrar, Dartmouth Leslie Center Lifeline's Poetry Share, Houston Library Poetry Share, Clamantis Journal, and the Dartmouth Medical School Lifeline's Journal. Al's collection, "Enter Atlas," was a Semi-Finalist for the University of Wisconsin's Brittingham & Felix Pollak Prizes in Poetry, judged by Natasha Trethewey. Al also plays the electric violin and enjoys making people laugh.

Al's poetry page can be viewed at PoetryByAlan.com
Twitter and Instagram: PoetryByAlan
Contact email: AASalehi@ucla.edu

Born in Brooklyn, NY, and raised in a Jewish-American family, **Ivy Schweitzer** has lived in Vermont for many years and taught courses in American Literature and Women and Gender Studies at Dartmouth College. She has recently published poetry in Bloodroot Literary Magazine, Antiphon volume 19, Clear Poetry, Passager, Ritualwell, Tikkun, New Croton Review, Mississippi Review, and Spoon River Poetry Review. In 2018, she felt called by Emily Dickinson to spend a year immersed in that poet's most creative period in which she wrote almost a poem a day; the result is a year-long weekly blog called White Heat: Emily Dickinson in 1862.
https://journeys.dartmouth.edu/whiteheat

Please visit her author page:
https://sites.dartmouth.edu/ivyschweitzer
Contact email: Ivy.Schweitzer@dartmouth.edu

Praise for *Within Flesh*

With brilliant wordplay, personal reflections, and Salehi's innovative "Senku," these brave poets peel back the surfaces of prejudice and injustice to expose that the nature of our issues are not black or white, but in fact, "Matters of Red." They place their fingers on the pulse of human compassion, illustrating that we are but one interconnected and interdependent organ. Ultimately, Al, Ivy, and Emily Dickinson joined verses to successfully prove that beneath our differences, there is heart— *Within Flesh*. —**Dr. Amir Najafi**; Diplomate, American Board of Interventional Cardiology

Emily Dickinson was always in dialogue. She asked a question, the Universe answered. They talked a bit. She wrote it down. Lives were changed. Al Salehi and Ivy Schweitzer are in dialogue with themselves, with Emily Dickinson, and the Universe. They wrote it down. Lives will change. For the better. *Within Flesh* will make you think, feel, and be alive. What more could you ask? —**Peter M. Webster**; Poet & Director of Dartmouth College's Vocal Performance Lab

Within Flesh is a striking reminder of the human condition's universality and that the seemingly insatiable fight to be heard reverberates cross-generationally. Al, Ivy, and Emily Dickinson, venture into a dynamic conversation that denotes the ubiquity of human introspection and sentimentality. They show that while our emotions are individually nuanced—our sorrows, desires, anger, happiness, and insecurities converge after "Realizing the Multichromatic Rainbow," arching over all members of humanity. This luminous collection of poems interacts with Dickinson's philosophies and grievances, skillfully applying an adaptive lens to magnify the similar socio-political struggles between the past generations. Through protest and poetry, Al and Ivy argue that our differing backgrounds, colors, and experiences, are not conditions sufficient to draw us apart—for we should be collectively conscious of the fact that "we all rebrand / as salt of the Earth." —**Paria Honardoust**; Poet & author of *Medusa's Mourning*

From time to time, we may lose our faith in humankind. These philosophers make the case for why we must always fight, relentlessly, "to embrace all humanity as a resolute act." Three different writing styles, cultures, and generations—this collection will certainly have something for everyone. *Within Flesh* is a work of art, brilliantly designed, from cover to cover. The interwoven fabric of poems by Al and Ivy is seamless and truly masterful! —**Xena Aziminia**; Professor of Design and Illustration, Otis College of Art and Design

What makes this book particularly intriguing is the dual experience that it offers its readers. It allows us to delve into the minds of the poets themselves, exploring how Emily Dickinson served as a catalyst for their expressions of remembrance, anger, sorrow, despair, and determination. These poems also afford us a historical perspective. As we contemplate Al and Ivy's activism through their powerful words, we are prompted to consider the differences, similarities, and changes in politics, racial tensions, and artistic expression over time. Their poetry is powerful and thought-provoking, particularly those that express indignation and anger while also touching on universal themes of morality, pain, and hope. There is certainly no holding back here! This collection is as bold and fresh as it is gorgeous and contemplative. Ultimately, *Within Flesh* is an achievement that will leave its readers captivated. —**Simona Moroni**; author of *Hollywood Daze*

Whether it be by the tapestry of beautifully woven refrain poetry or by the succinct Salehi "Senku," you will find yourself mesmerized by the end of this collection. Interacting with Emily Dickinson's writings, Al and Ivy reimagine and reframe her insight for today's readers. Their poems are jaw-droppingly clever as they are two highly intelligent creatives, who have seamlessly united to delve into language, politics and what matters now, by considering what mattered then. Their craft is of the highest caliber elucidating nuanced ideas of Self-Determination. *Within Flesh* takes steps beyond usual literary confines with a sincere and unified voice, calling for reconciliation and equity. These exceptional poets have truly created a timeless masterpiece! —**Candice Louisa Daquin**; Senior Editor, *Indie Blu(e) Publishing*, Editorial Associate, *Raw Earth Ink*

Made in the USA
Middletown, DE
05 April 2024

52476585R00078